Ink, Fire & Silence

The Ones Who Taught, The Battles That Burned, and What Remains

Dr. Bitumani Borah

Dedication

To the poet who taught me how to see:
not just with my eyes,
but with the silence between heartbeats.
To William Wordsworth,
and to every golden daffodil that still blooms in the
memory of a child.

For the souls who shaped me.. some with love, some
with pain, and some with silence.

For the battles I fought, the lessons I learned, and the
fires that never died.

For the teen girl in the ICU, the woman in making I see
in the mirror daily, and the voices that were never
heard.. this is for you

For those who are suffering silently (such as in an ICU)
or in silence

Preface

"Ink, Fire & Silence" is not just a collection of poems; it is a journey.. one that traverses the landscapes of illness, resilience, heartbreak, friendship, and self-discovery.

Some souls come into our lives to love us, others to challenge us, and some to leave us with lessons we never saw coming. This book is woven with the echoes of those who shaped me through silence, through fire, and through their undeniable presence in my story.

Acknowledgements

I would not have been able to bring this book to life without the souls who have, knowingly or unknowingly, shaped me.

Family – The First Foundation

To my papa. Your unwavering presence in my darkest days taught me resilience. You became my voice when I had none, and without words, you understood everything.

To my mummy. The lessons you taught me, though difficult, molded me into the woman I am today. Strictness and discipline teaches in its own way.

To my daughter, Honey bee as I call her that affectionately. You are my greatest reason to keep going. My fiercest love, my loudest laughter, my purest purpose. May you grow up knowing that strength is not about how many times you fall but how fiercely you rise.

To Hiramoni Didi, Dipti, Borta, Borma, Raju Bhaiya, Deepu Bhaiya, Grace Bhabhi, and my mother-in-law. You proved that family isn't always born. Sometimes, it's built. You held space for me in ways that mattered when it mattered the most.

Career – Growth Through Fire and Lessons

To the College of Veterinary Science, Assam. It taught me resilience in its rawest form. Five years of rigorous learning, two years of NCC, and lessons that extended far beyond textbooks. It forced me to break my own limitations, to push my body and mind beyond what I believed possible. It was not just an education. It was survival, growth, and transformation.

To James (JD), my first boss, who introduced me to the relentless world of door-to-door fundraising in England. Knocking on doors in the bone-chilling environment of the UK, advocating for a cause that mattered, the importance of first aid in schools. It was more than just a job; it was a lesson in persistence, in believing in something enough to face closed doors over and over again. I learned that rejection is just redirection, that if you don't ask, you don't get, and that resilience isn't built in comfort but in discomfort.

To my ex boss James, who gave me the opportunity to dive into the world of neurological and immunological diseases. This journey of learning has been transformative, connecting my professional knowledge to personal experiences in ways I never expected. It continues to shape my understanding of science and its impact on lives.

To the University of Manchester, the University of Salford, and Keele University. Studying my master's with scholarship at premier institutions of the world was not just an academic achievement; it was a deeper dive into the world of biology and science, a journey that made me question, analyze, and understand the intricate connections between the body and mind. Science became more than knowledge. It became a way to make sense of my own survival.

To my colleagues. The ones who became my biggest cheerleaders, who reminded me of my worth when I forgot, who celebrated my wins as if they were their own. You know who you are.

Love, Absence, and the Ones Who Shaped Me

To Ashish. You were the foundation beneath my feet, even when the walls around me felt hollow. Absence has a presence of its own, and in ways the world will never understand, you were there. A shadow, a structure, a stability wrapped in distance.

To the ones who arrived like fire and left like whispers. The ones who stayed in the silence. The ones who saw me, understood me, and, in their own way, changed me. Some connections defy time, logic, and even reason. This book carries pieces of you too.

Friendship – The Chosen Family

To Ravi Uncle and the departed soul of Kumud Auntie. Your lives, your wisdom, and the quiet, powerful ways in which you existed in this world continue to guide me. Some people leave, yet never truly go.

To my girls' gang. You know who you are. You are the laughter in my chaos, the calm in my storm, the proof that friendship is the greatest love story of all. This book carries echoes of you, your words, your presence.

For the Reader

To every soul who reads these words. This book is as much yours as it is mine. If you have ever battled loss, faced limitations, or questioned the lessons life throws your way, know that you are not alone.

To BookLeaf Publications. This challenge became more

than just 21 days of writing. It became a reckoning, a reflection, and a release.

Thank you.

1. Section 1: The Silence That Spoke First

Chapter 1: Breathing Without Sound

"When your body forgets how to speak for you, you begin to speak through pain, breath, and sheer will. These are the sounds I made, without a single word."

Survival is often seen as a triumph, a victory against the odds. But what if survival comes with silence? What if the body refuses to move, the voice refuses to rise, and the only way to communicate is through a blink?

This chapter takes you into the heart of the ICU, where machines dictate life, where pain is endured without protest, and where the struggle is not just against illness but against invisibility. It is a space where breath is borrowed, where hands heal and hurt in the same motion, where the line between life and limbo blurs.

The poems in this section are not just about medical battles but about the war of being unheard. They explore the terror of power cuts when machines hold your life in their circuits, the helplessness of feeling pain but being unable to express it, and the slow, suffocating wait for a body to listen again.

Through blink-based communication, hallucinations that teeter between comfort and fear, and a father who becomes both soldier and savior, these verses uncover the quiet agony of existing without control, of fighting without moving, of screaming without sound.

These poems are a testament to resilience.. not the loud, celebrated kind, but the silent, relentless kind. The kind that teaches you to fight even when no one is listening.

"When reality fades, the mind invites shadows to keep you company."

Prologue: "When Words Were Stolen"

I was born in the capital of India twice.

Once in an army hospital, wrapped in warmth,
and again, years later, in a sterile ICU,
where silence was my first breath of life.
I woke up in a world where silence screamed,
where my body lay still, a stranger to me.
Trapped inside, I blinked at the void,
a prisoner in flesh, forgotten by time.

The air smelled of antiseptic and fear,
machines hummed where my voice should be.
Fingers twitched in a dream, but not in life,
lungs borrowed breath from tubes and wires.
A ventilator breathed for me,
rhythmic, mechanical, cold.

My own breath was a whisper lost in the void,
lungs too weak to claim the air as mine.
They called it survival,
but survival came with a price.
A heart swollen with struggle,
a body at war with itself.

Eight, ten, more,
faces I never saw, voices I never knew,
hands that fought to keep me tethered,
doctors, specialists, strangers writing my fate.
And then the power cut.

The beeping stopped, the hum disappeared,
and suddenly, hands rushed, frantic, firm.
The ambu bag squeezed, air forced, pain rising.
Minutes stretched into eternity.

Pain in places I didn't know existed.
I couldn't cry out, couldn't beg them to stop,
could only endure, only exist.
Fifteen days, no movement, no release,
a body holding everything inside,
organs waiting, pressing, aching,
and still, they said, patience.
In the capital of a country that never sleeps,
I was locked in a body that never moved.

They came and went,
white coats, shifting shadows, decisions made above my
head.
But not every touch was meant to heal.
Some hands lingered where they shouldn't.
Rough fingers pressed where there was no consent,
a violation whispered in the hush of routine.
I screamed inside a body that wouldn't move,
shouted into silence, begged my own flesh to wake.
But my voice had been stolen,
and no one heard what was never spoken.

But not everything was real.
Not everything was flesh and bone.
Somewhere between the morphine and the stillness,
a ghost sat by my side.
It whispered stories only I could hear,
It's presence flickering in the corners of my sight.
It kept me scared, it kept me sane,
a friend, a fear, an illusion I refused to lose.
Then, in the quiet, someone else stayed.

Not a doctor, not a nurse, not a shadow passing by.
A presence, unseen, yet certain,
watching, waiting, knowing.
Did they hear the words trapped in my throat?
Did they know the war behind my eyes?
A whisper brushed against my mind,
"I see you."
And for the first time, I was not alone.

2. Blink, and the World Moved

He stood beside me, steady as steel,
a jawan who was serving the Indian Air Force,
waging a different kind of war,
a battle for my voice, my choice, my will.

They thought I was voiceless,
that silence had swallowed me whole,
but my father knew better.
A soldier never surrenders,
and neither would his daughter.

He recited the alphabet,
steady, patient, waiting.
A. B. C. D...
My eyes would hold on the right letter,
and the world would move at my command.
N-nurse.
D-doctor.

M-mummy.
S-change my side.
They said I couldn't speak,
but I spelled my way back to existence.
They said I couldn't ask,
but my father made sure I was heard.

Even warriors kneel for their daughters,
and even without sound,
a father will always hear.

3. The Language of Shadows

I was never alone in that room,
though my body lay still, unseen, unheard.
Machines whispered in electric hums,
footsteps faded in and out,
but something else remained.

A shadow sat at the edge of my sight,
not flesh, not machine, not memory.
It spoke in half-formed whispers,
stories I wasn't sure were mine.

The nurses saw nothing.
The doctors measured nothing.
But I knew,
between the morphine and the quiet,
someone watched.

Some nights, it was a friend,
an unseen voice spinning tales,

keeping me from drowning in the silence.
Other nights, it was a phantom,
pulling me deeper into the unknown.

I couldn't run, couldn't fight,
trapped between dreams and waking.
Fear had no sound here,
only the cold weight of knowing
that I was not alone.

Was it death, waiting for me?
Or my own mind, desperate for company?
Perhaps both.
Perhaps neither.
Perhaps survival isn't just about lungs that breathe,
or hearts that beat,
but about making peace
with the ghosts that keep us alive.

4. The War Beneath My Skin

They called it survival,
but survival felt like war.
A battle fought in shadows,
where I was both the battlefield and the prisoner.

My lungs refused to claim the air,
tubes carried it instead,
each inhale borrowed,
each exhale forced.

My heart swelled, not with love,
but with the weight of struggle.
A machine dictated my rhythm,
pumping life into veins too weak to fight.

They worked in silence,
eight, ten, more...
doctors calculating, measuring, deciding.
I was the equation,
but no one asked if I wanted to be solved.

I was alive,
but I had never felt so far from living.

5. Between Power Cuts and Pain

The beeping stopped before the pain began.
A city that never slept went dark,
but inside these walls,
machines needed more than promises to stay alive.

The ventilator stilled.
A breath I had not taken disappeared,
stolen by silence.

Then hands..
frantic, firm, unrelenting.
The ambu bag pressed against me,
forcing air where my body refused.

Pain sliced through the fog,
each squeeze a reminder-
that survival was never gentle.

There were no lights,

no alarms,
just urgency,
just breath being pushed into unwilling and quiet lungs.
I could not cry out.
I could not beg them to stop.
Pain is different when you cannot run away from it.

The city moved on,
the lights flickered back,
but my body knew
there are some darknesses
that never truly leave.

6. Fifteen Days of Waiting

Time was an illusion in that room,
marked not by sunrises or sunsets,
but by shifts of faces,
by the rhythm of IV drips,
by the weight inside me that refused to leave.

Fifteen days.
Fifteen days without movement,
without release,
without the simple proof that my body still belonged to
me.

They measured everything..
my blood, my breath, my heart,
but not the growing pressure,
the slow ache,
the silent scream of a body waiting to be heard.
They said, patience.
That bodies adjust, that time will work.
But time does not move

when you are locked inside it.

I counted the days in blinks,
in unanswered prayers,
in the slow, suffocating wait
for my body to listen to me again.

And when it finally did,
it felt like another war had been won.

*"I survived the silence. But what saved me were the
voices that stayed."*

7. Chapter 2: Lifelines & The Ones Who Stayed

There are moments in life that don't just hurt... they halt
you. Guillain-Barré Syndrome did that to me. It stripped
me of movement, sound, and independence. But in that
stillness, some souls stood up for me. Some lifted, some
fought, and some simply stayed.

This chapter is a tribute to the people who did not need
to be asked. My borta, Raju bhaiya, deepu bhaiya who
sent borma to New Delhi to meet me in the ICU and to
be a great support system for my parents who were
trying to figure things out in a new place. My school
friends who became the scaffolding of my recovery..
completing assignments, visiting the hospital, sitting
quietly at my bedside. My teacher, Bhatnagar Ma'am,
who didn't just believe in me, she fought for my right to
return. And the Indian Army physiotherapists who
didn't see me as a case file, but as a girl who would walk
again, live again, and one day, hold her own child.

These are the lifelines I didn't choose, but who chose me. This chapter is for the ones who never flinched at my brokenness. Who stayed when staying was hard.

Section 1: School Friendships That Held Me Together

"When my legs couldn't carry me, their presence did."

Poem: They Walked So I Could

I couldn't walk,
but they never let me feel left behind.

Piyush, Tanmay, Dinesh,
Vandana, Shailendra, Anoop, Richa and those whom I
didn't name out..
they showed up with notebooks and hearts,
turned homework into healing,
and silence into solidarity.

While I blinked through pain,
they sat by my bedside,
finishing schoolwork and filling my room
with stories, greeting cards, flowers, chocolates, teddy
bears, smiles, and the kind of laughter
that made me believe I wasn't forgotten.

I didn't need to ask.
They just came.
And that's how I knew..
they were already my cure.

8. The Girl Who Couldn't Move

“*Sometimes the loudest ‘I love you’ is someone showing
up without needing to be asked.*”

I was a girl who couldn't move,
yet the world around me
never stayed still.
Friends who brought stories from school,
hands that combed my hair,
and eyes that told me
I was still one of them.

They didn't ask how I felt.
They already knew.
They didn't say it would be okay.
They made sure it was.
They were my motion
when I had none.
My belonging
when I had lost all rhythm.

9. Section 2: Mentors Who Fought Quietly

"Some teachers don't just educate. They protect your future when you can't fight for it yourself."

Poem: Bhatnagar Ma'am

She didn't teach from the textbook.
She taught from belief.

When the rules said no,
she walked into the principal's room
with her calm voice
and fierce insistence.

Give her a re-exam.
Give her a chance.
She will rise.
She will return.

No debate.

Just quiet conviction.

She never told me I could do it.
She just made sure
no one else said I couldn't.

10. Section 3: Bodies, Battles & Breakthroughs

"The first person who believed I'd walk again didn't need proof.. he needed purpose."

Poem: March Orders from a Soldier's Hands

They said I might never walk again.
But the Indian Army doesn't believe in never.

One look,
one nod,
and my new physiotherapist
declared war on doubt.

This wasn't therapy.
This was discipline.
This was duty.

Every rep was a battle,

every stretch a salute
to a future they believed in
even when I couldn't.

To them,
if I could walk,
I could finish school.
If I could finish school,
I could build a life.
If I could build a life,
I could become a mother.

And so, they made me march.

"Healing isn't always medical. Sometimes it's emotional
weight redistributed by those who refuse to let you
collapse"

Poem: Hands That Carried My Future

Some hands healed,
some lifted,
some just held on.

My parents watched me fade,
but never let me go.
My friends carried schoolbags

and smiles I didn't know I needed.
My teachers wrote my name
into rooms I wasn't in
just to keep me from being erased.

They carried me
when I couldn't carry myself..
not just in distance,
but through time.

"Even when nothing was moving on the outside, love
kept everything alive inside me."

Poem: Healing in the Absence of Movement

I lay still for days
but healing was never still.

It moved through voices at my window,
through friends laughing beside my bed,
through stories of school assemblies
and class gossip whispered like lifelines.

It came through eyes that didn't pity,
through hands that didn't flinch.
It came in waves..
unmeasured by progress,

but full of quiet faith.

They never asked if I was tired.
They just reminded me
that I was still here.
Still me.

11. Section 4: Love That Arrived Without Bloodlines

"Some journeys don't begin with birth.. they begin with choice, courage, and an unshakable bond."

Poem: The Ones Who Weren't Bound By Blood

News travelled fast..
faster than my strength could fade.
And in a city far away,
hearts broke quietly in Bangalore.
Deepu Bhaiya,
who'd seen the world in camera lights,
held his grief in trembling hands
and turned it into action.
He placed a cap and bag from his company
in Borma's gentle hands,
a woman with no map,
only courage stitched into her saree pleats.

She flew across cities,
not for herself,
but for me.
For my parents.
For the friendship that began in the 90s
and never once asked
whether it was enough to be called family.
Borta watched with a silent ache.
Raju Bhaiya couldn't hold back tears.
No one said "why us."
They only said..
"Tell us where to be."

Not blood,
but something deeper.
Not kin,
but the kind of love
that shows up without needing to be named.

*"I was placed like cargo, but remembered like kin. That
contrast still holds the heaviest weight in my chest."*

Poem: Not Carried, But Dragged
They laid me on the floor of a train,
not on a stretcher,

not with dignity,
just a bed pushed between aisles,
as if I were baggage
and not a school girl slowly fading.

No food.
No water.
No words of comfort.
Just the hum of Shatabdi's wheels
and the ache of being nothing more
than a body to be moved.

I was dying on that floor,
but no one could see me.. not really.
They saw weakness,
not worth.

And yet..
on the way back,
when healing had begun to whisper,
I lay on a bed again.. still still,
but this time,
something had shifted.
Not in my spine,
but in my soul.

And when we reached Agra again,

Dutta Uncle and Aunty,
not bound by blood,
had filled the Air Force quarter
with flowers and messages..
"Get well soon" pinned like prayers
on walls that remembered who I had been.

No one had to do any of it.
But they did.
And it reminded me..
I may have been carried like cargo,
but I was never unloved.

*"The world moves forward because someone still
chooses to show up with flowers, for no reason other
than love."*

Poem: The World Was Held Together Quietly
While I lay still in hospital beds,
there were homes that opened without being asked.
In New Delhi's Air Force quarters,
in Agra's army corridors,
uniforms turned into kindness,
and ranks bowed to love.
Fauji families became our pulse—

bringing meals,
offering company,
sitting with my parents in silence
that needed no explaining.

And my uncle,
gently preparing food
with the precision of love,
feeding not just our bodies
but the faith that healing would come.

We think the world moves through noise,
but it is these quiet, unseen hands
that keep it spinning.

Not in speeches or ceremonies,
but in rotis shared,
beds adjusted,
and tears witnessed by strangers
who became family
because that's what humanity looks like
when it chooses to care.

12. Section 5: Reflections Shared and Remembered

"It took a microphone and memory to understand.. healing isn't just what happened. It's what stayed."

Poem: I Didn't Realize Until I Spoke It

It took years
and the safety of stranger's microphone
for me to say their names aloud
without breaking.

Aditya and Dr. Shreya,
My two podcasters,
One from Mumbai,
Another from New Delhi.
Who ensured that my journey of severe GBS is heard
First in layman's language
And another in a more structured
Medical manner.

GBS was on rise
And it was no surprise.
Ankita shook me,
Told me to raise my voice.
She redirected me to Wrisha,
The amazing Bollywood singer!
Who became my hearts harbinger.

Connected me to Aditya,
The Ray of hope and light.
He further showed me a more specific path,
Dr. Shreya,
Who calls me Bee affectionately ❤

I spoke of notebooks filled by other hands,
of hospital beds surrounded by teenage laughter,
of a teacher who stood taller than fear.

I hadn't planned to cry.
But sometimes healing catches you off guard
not when it happens,
but when you remember it did.

They were just children then.
But they held space for me
like they had known grief

and chose kindness anyway.

And somewhere between
Those podcast questions
and my trembling answers,
I realized..
they didn't just help me survive.
They taught me what love sounds like
when it doesn't need to be loud.

"Not all lifelines are loud. Some arrive quietly, sit beside you without a word, and stay long after the pain forgets your name"

13. Chapter 3: Love in the Grey

Section: The Many Forms of Almost

Note
Some of us survive illness.
Some of us survive loss.
And some of us...
survive the kind of love
that never made it to the surface.

This chapter is for those
who suffered silently
not just in their bodies,
but in their hearts.
For those who waited quietly,
who carried what they couldn't claim,
who left with dignity,
but never really let go.

Love in the grey is not loud.
It doesn't come with labels.
It doesn't stay long enough to be called forever.
But it leaves something behind..
a lesson,
a longing,
a version of yourself you wouldn't have met otherwise.

You don't have to name it to honour it.
You don't have to explain it to feel it.
You just have to let it live where it belongs..
softly,
in the grey.

Poem: He Wasn't the First
He wasn't the first
to hold me in his silence.
But he was the first
to make my silence feel held.

There was one who steadied the storm
not with presence,
but with predictability.
He stayed,
even when he didn't show up.

Another arrived like a spark,
too bright to belong
in the life I'd built around duty.
He gave nothing,
yet I lost pieces of myself
in his everything.

And then there was the one
who looked at me
like I wasn't hard to love.
Only hard to keep.

They never met.
They never knew.
But each left something
in the grey space between
what I needed
and what I chose.

14. The Man Who Didn't Say It

He never said he loved me.
Not once.
But he remembered things
I didn't know I'd said
because it made it easier
to find his way back
when he needed warmth
without commitment.

He'd send a message
after a long silence
not with explanations,
but just enough breadcrumbs
to lead me back into maybe.

He never asked me to wait.
But every time I tried to leave,
he left a door open
just wide enough

to trip over again.

Sometimes,
manipulation is gentle.
Sometimes,
it wears the scent of love
and the timing of absence.

15. The One Who Chose Stability

He was always there.
Reliable.
Predictable.
Absent in all the ways
that don't make headlines
but still leave bruises.

He brought groceries
but never curiosity.
He stayed in the room
but never entered my mind.

He didn't hurt me.
But he made sure
I forgot
how it felt to be held
by someone who sees you
instead of simply standing next to you.

16. Coffee That Went Cold

It wasn't a grand goodbye.
It was missed calls,
seen-but-unread texts,
and conversations
that stopped meaning anything
but kept happening anyway.

He stayed long enough
to keep me hopeful,
but never long enough
to build anything real.

His exit was quiet
but his pattern wasn't.
I later found out
he was practicing
the same kind of softness
on someone else.

Sometimes the coldest thing

is not that they left
but that you know
they've done this before.
And they'll do it again.

17. Parallel Lives

We had the same dreams
but yours had fine print.
And exit plans.
And doors that locked from your side.

You wanted forever,
but only if it didn't ask
for real presence.

I wanted love,
not strategy.
You gave half-truths
dressed as emotional depth.

I gave trust
to someone still auditioning.

We weren't wrong.
We just weren't honest.

Not at the same time.

Not even to ourselves.

18. The Pause Between Messages

There's a rhythm to us.
You vanish.
I ache.
You return.
I forgive myself
for answering again.

We don't talk about it.
We just press repeat.
Like it isn't a pattern.
Like it isn't manipulation
with a smile.

You mastered
just enough silence
to make me crave
your crumbs like a feast.

There were no promises.

Just pauses.
Just control
in softer clothes.

And still,
I reply.
But this time,
it costs you something, too.

19. All the Names I Don't Say

I write about you,
and you,
and the one who believed
silence was a strategy.
I fold your patterns
into poetry
so the world thinks
I'm still in love
when I'm just...
making sure no one else
falls for the same script.
Your hands
became metaphors.
Your messages
became mirrors
I won't look into anymore.

No, I won't say your name.
Not because I care

but because it doesn't deserve
a single page more.

20. What Almost Meant

It meant long nights
filled with almost-apologies.
It meant half-promises,
crafted with full confidence.
It meant never letting go,
and never holding on
a perfect balancing act
of emotional convenience.

It meant me
trying to make a home
out of borrowed hours
and stolen attention.

You never said it was love.
But you behaved
just close enough
for me to question
my own boundaries.

Now I know.

Almost
was just the shape
your selfishness wore
when it needed
to feel sacred.

21. Section 6: Unwritten Echoes

Ashes, Ink & the Quiet After (a soft exhale at the end of a storm)

Note

This isn't a conclusion.
It's a quiet continuation.
I didn't write these poems to close my wounds.
I wrote them so they wouldn't close me.
Every page in this book was peeled from a place I never
thought I'd speak of again
ICU silences, interrupted childhoods, half-held hands,
losses that never had funerals, and
love that taught me how deeply one can ache

without a sound.

This final chapter is not about survival.
It's about what remains
after you've survived.

It's about what still pulses
when the noise ends
the breath after the scream,
the stillness after the fire,
the ink that dries without apology.

Poem 1: What They Didn't See
They saw the return.
Not the crawl back.
They saw the stage.
Not the hospital corners I bit my tongue through.

They saw the confidence.
Not the nights I practiced breathing
like it was a skill to be relearned.

They saw the book.
Not the trembling hands
that wrote it.

Poem 2: The Girl With the Blink Code
She never spoke,
but she screamed through letters.
'N' for nurse.
'D' for doctor.
'M' for mummy.
'A' for side.

She blinked her way
back into the world.
And they still underestimate
what she can do
with just her eyes.

Poem 3: What Fire Taught Me
Not all flames burn.
Some cleanse.
Some melt away
what was never meant to survive.

The fire didn't ruin me.
It revealed me.

I wasn't reborn in light.
I was remade in heat.
That's why I glow
differently now.

Poem 4: Ashes Don't Apologize
I don't regret who I became
after everything broke.
I don't owe softness
to those who mistook my silence
for surrender.

I'm not the girl
who waits for someone to believe her.
I'm the woman
who published her pain
in permanent ink.

Poem 5: The Pages I Didn't Write
There are still poems
I couldn't write.
Still memories
too raw for even poetry.

Like what it felt like
to be touched
when I couldn't move.

Like the exact moment

I stopped trusting hands
that weren't mine.

But maybe the point
isn't to write everything.
Maybe the power
is in what I didn't give away.

Poem 6: When I Finally Stopped Explaining
There came a day
I stopped writing for people
who asked for proof.
For understanding.
For justification.

I stopped explaining
why I stayed.
Why I left.
Why I cried.
Why I kept loving anyway.

And suddenly,
my voice felt like mine again.

Poem 7: This Book Isn't Just Mine

This isn't a dedication.
It's a permission slip.
To the woman
reading this in secret.
To the girl
who still thinks her voice is too much.
To the man
who loved in silence
and lost himself there.

This book is yours too
if you've ever held on quietly,
loved too gently,
or fought to return
to a body
that didn't feel like home.

Poem 8: Ink, Fire & Silence
Ink gave me memory.
Fire gave me rage.
Silence gave me peace.

This book was never just poetry.
It was a resurrection.
Of voice.
Of self.

Of soul.

Final Reflection: And Still, She Rises
Not every battle was visible.
Not every wound bled.
But every piece of me
that made it to these pages
fought to be here.

I have faced
illness
paralysis
molestation
rejection
emotional starvation
and the ache of half-held love.

But I have also known
unseen loyalty,
friendships that held me like blood never could,
and teachers who gave me futures
without asking for thank-yous.
And somehow,
through it all,
I've managed to heal,
to work,

to parent,
to love,
and still smile with my entire face
a smile that holds both
what I've carried
and what I've let go.

I may never be done
with healing.

But I am done
with hiding.

This isn't the end.
It's just where I stop whispering
and let the world
read what I was always afraid to say out loud.

Looking Ahead: A Soft Promise
There's more to come.

The next book will speak of the things
I've only hinted at here
a deeper dive into what it means
to keep showing up
with grace

after every quiet undoing.

I'll talk about
the weight of caregiving,
the fire in motherhood,
what it feels like to raise joy
while managing pain,
and the quiet strength
of not letting your story define your softness.

Because survival is not a final chapter.
It's a genre of its own.

And I'm still writing it.

Unwritten Echoes

Introduction:

The journey didn't end when the book did.
There were still echoes to be heard,
stories to be told,
and miles to be crossed.
Some paths weren't planned.
Some were forced.
Some were chosen with trembling hands
and an iron will.

And in the middle of all that chaos,
I kept writing.
Because ink, fire, and silence
are not things you can simply lay down.
They are threads you keep weaving,
even when the world says it's time to stop.
This section holds the untold chapters,
the days that almost broke me,
and the journeys that built me.

Chapter: Crazy March 2025

March 2025 was nothing short of a whirlwind: a chaotic,
fast-paced dance of travel, work, and motherhood. It was

a month that demanded resilience and meticulous planning, yet somehow, amidst the madness, there were moments of beauty and grace.

The Mumbai-Pune-Mumbai Rush

It all began on March 6th with a one-day trip from Pune to Mumbai. The purpose? To submit assets from my previous organization at their Patalganga office. Ashish drove me there, and I was grateful for his time and effort. To thank him, I treated him to Pasha at JW Marriott, a small gesture for his generosity.

The Vistadome Experience

Just two days later, on March 8th, I embarked on a mesmerizing journey from Pune to Hyderabad on the Shatabdi Vistadome train. The panoramic views were stunning, and the journey felt like a much-needed breath of fresh air. I had officially joined my new organization on March 10th, and the energy of a fresh beginning was intoxicating.

I returned from Hyderabad to Pune on March 17th, boarding a 4:30 am flight. The sleepless night made the following day at the office in Pune challenging but manageable.

Back to Hyderabad Again

My second trip to Hyderabad began on March 23rd,

prompted by a stakeholder visit. I once again took the Shatabdi train, relishing the journey even amidst work pressures. This time, I returned to Pune on March 28th, catching a 4:30 am flight and landing just in time to make it to my daughter's school.

Collecting her progress report, meeting her teachers, and celebrating her last day at school felt like the real highlight of the month. Those small moments with her were precious, especially amidst all the chaos.

Medicon Madness

The intensity of my new role was unlike anything I had experienced before. I was assigned to lead a pilot Medicon conference with an almost impossible turnaround time: 48 hours for 40+ sessions streaming live in Chicago. Coordinating efforts across the globe, from the Global, South East Asia, India Region, and China, was nothing short of monumental.

The team comprised principal writers, expert writers, senior writers, graphic designers, and content managers. Three stakeholders, a short turnaround time, and a relentless work schedule became the norm. But I thrived in it, pushing myself and the team to make the seemingly impossible possible.

Chapter: The Kolhapur Journey

He drives 14 hours every month to the Kolhapur
#Shaktipeeth,
A pilgrimage of devotion and effort,
Where wheels turn and roads stretch,
A journey woven in ritual and routine.
He is there for her, present in ways he wasn't before,
A father more grounded, taking visual efforts to
connect.
Bedside coffee arrives sometimes, warm but not always,
Like gestures made of comfort, missing something
intangible.
He brings small gifts occasionally, tokens of
thoughtfulness,
Moments where he acknowledges the hard work I put
in.
Tiny efforts that whisper of care,
Yet the echoes still feel distant.
Efforts now are clearer, like sketches filled with color,
But the hues still fall short of painting wholeness.
It's progress, not fulfillment.
Kindness, not intimacy.
Presence, not depth.
The road to Kolhapur remains constant.
The journey between us remains unfinished.

Chapter: Unwritten Echoes

Reflection:

I once thought survival was the finish line.

Now I see it's just a checkpoint..

a place to rest,

not to stop.

I have faced:

- Illnesses that tried to silence me.
- Molestation that tried to break me.
- Exhaustion that tried to erase me.
- Betrayals that left scars where trust should have been.
- Friendships that held me like blood never could.
- Lover who never truly loved but still left their mark.
- Jobs that drained me and roles that redefined me.

And still, I rose.

Not because I healed completely,

but because I kept moving

even when the ground trembled.

There will be more Crazy Marches.

More Kolhapur Journeys.

More battles to fight,

and more moments to savor.

This book doesn't end here.

It only pauses.

For you.
For me.
For everything we're still learning how to carry.

Looking Ahead: A Soft Promise

This isn't the end.
This is just the beginning.
The next book will speak of the battles I've only hinted
at here,
the quiet griefs, the everyday wars, the peace I had to
learn how to make.
It will unravel what it means to carry the weight of
caregiving,
to raise joy while managing pain,
to remain graceful under pressure,
and to keep smiling with a gorgeous strength
even when the world insists on crumbling around me.
I am still writing.
I am still healing.
And I am still here.

The Child Who Saw Daffodils (Final chapter)

A closing chapter for the ones who still believe in wonder

In 2011, long before I wore all the labels this life handed me: survivor, author, mother, woman stitched with silence and fire, I was walking door-to-door in the Lake District, fundraising for St. John Ambulance.

It was not glamorous work. But it was honest. Soulful.
Barefoot, in a way.
Each knock on a stranger's door came with a sky full of questions and an occasional smile that warmed me more than any English sun ever could.

I stayed in **Ambleside** for a month.
Not in passing.
I *lived* there: walked by the lakes, climbed the gentle green of the hills, and paused often just to breathe.
The silence there didn't feel empty.
It felt like company.

And it was **cold**.
Not the cold that bites once and lets go:

but the kind that seeps into your bones and lingers.
The skies often wept. The rain fell like mist and memory.
And I, a girl from a hot country, wrapped in all the
layers I had,
stood there: soaking wet some days, freezing most:
and still knocked on doors.
Still smiled. Still spoke. Still stood.

Because I was there for a cause.
Because when you walk with purpose, even the wind
steps aside.
And because: I always have been, and always will be,
my own backup.

One weekend, I made my way to **Cockermouth**.
The birthplace of **William Wordsworth**.
The same poet whose verses I had read in school in
classes 7, 8, and 9.
Back when I didn't fully understand grief, or strength,
or solitude: but somehow, through his words, I
understood *beauty*.
That it could be quiet.
That it could be simple.
That it could heal.

I visited the Georgian house where he was born.
I think they called it Wordsworth House.

I walked through it like one walks through a childhood
dream: half-remembered, half-etched in emotion.
And in that moment, I wasn't a fundraiser or a traveler.
I was the little girl again, holding her schoolbook, falling
in love with *Daffodils*.
Here's the poem that started it all for me:

Daffodils

by William Wordsworth

I wandered lonely as a cloud
That floats on high o'er vales and hills,
When all at once I saw a crowd,
A host, of golden daffodils;
Beside the lake, beneath the trees,
Fluttering and dancing in the breeze.

Continuous as the stars that shine
And twinkle on the milky way,
They stretched in never-ending line
Along the margin of a bay:
Ten thousand I saw at a glance,
Tossing their heads in sprightly dance.

The waves beside them danced; but they
Out-did the sparkling waves in glee:
A poet could not but be gay,

In such a jocund company:
I gazed—and gazed—but little thought
What wealth the show to me had brought:

For oft, when on my couch I lie
In vacant or in pensive mood,
They flash upon that inward eye
Which is the bliss of solitude;
And then my heart with pleasure fills,
And dances with the daffodils.

When I first read those lines as a child, I didn't know
what solitude meant.
But I knew how it felt to dance with something beautiful
in my mind again and again.
Years later, lying on hospital beds, trapped inside my
body, fighting back tears in silence, I would close my
eyes: and there they were.
The daffodils.
Still fluttering.
Still dancing.
Still mine.

I admire the world around me because I know how
fragile it is.
How easily it can all be taken away.
But also: how it can return, suddenly and gloriously,

with just a line, a memory, or a flower.

The gardens I passed in Ambleside.
The moss-covered stones.
The soft lilac tulips peeking out beside doorsteps.
The waterfall hidden behind trees, its sound echoing like
a secret.
The winding roads that bent like a poet's verse.

I hold them all within me.
And now, through this chapter: maybe, you do too.

This chapter is not about poetry.
It is about presence.
It is about the parts of us that still wonder.
Still wander.
Still believe that golden things can bloom in the darkest
corners of our mind.

I was just a girl
who read a poem
and learned how to see.
And maybe, in some way,
I still am.

"Poetry begins where certainty ends:
in the soft space where wonder teaches us how to see
again."

from Ink, Fire & Silence

Now it's your turn to write. ♥